A HISTORICAL ALBUM OF
WASHINGTON

A HISTORICAL ALBUM OF

WASHINGTON

William Cocke

THE MILLBROOK PRESS, Brookfield, Connecticut

Front and back cover: "Mount St. Helens," painting by Paul Kane, 1847. Courtesy of the Stark Museum of Art, Texas.

Title page: The Cascade Mountains. Courtesy Olympic National Park.

Library of Congress Cataloging-in-Publication Data

Cocke, William. 1960–
     A historical album of Washington / by William Cocke.
          p.   cm. — (Historical albums)
     Includes bibliographical references and index.
     Summary: A history of Washington, from its early exploration
and settlement to the state today.
     ISBN 1-56294-508-4 (lib. bdg.)   ISBN 1-56294-851-2 (pbk.)
     1. Washington (State)—History—Juvenile literature. 2. Washington
(State)—Gazetteers—Juvenile literature. [1. Washington (State)—History.]
I. Title. II. Series.
F891.3.C63 1995
979.7—dc20   94-39256
                                                                     CIP
                                                                      AC

 Created in association with Media Projects Incorporated

C. Carter Smith, *Executive Editor*
Lelia Wardwell, *Managing Editor*
William Cocke, *Principal Writer*
Bernard Schleifer, *Art Director*
Shelley Latham, *Production Editor*
Arlene Goldberg, *Cartographer*

Consultant: Donald P. King, Professor & Chair, Dept. of History, Whitman College.

Manufactured in the United States of America

10 9 8 7 6 5 4 3 2 1

CONTENTS

Introduction

The state of Washington, named in honor of America's first president, was one of this country's last frontiers. Geographically, it is a land of great beauty and many contrasts. The Cascade Mountains divide the state from north to south, giving its western and eastern halves dramatically different climates and landscapes. Western Washington is a land of dense forests, heavy rainfall and a dramatic Pacific coastline.

The eastern half of Washington is much drier and flatter. It is made up of areas so dry they qualify as deserts and the Columbia Basin, a region of rich, rolling farmland. Through the entire state runs the Columbia River, one of the mightiest rivers in the West.

Washington has had a rich and colorful history. The Native American tribes in Washington first made contact with Europeans in the 18th century. Explorers from Spain and England arrived by sea. Later hunters, trappers, and explorers from the young United States came by land. Their accounts of the region's abundant natural resources prompted traders and pioneers to head to Washington. By the early 1800s, an extensive fur-trade network stretched along the coast of the Pacific Northwest. Missionaries followed the fur traders, and they, in turn, were followed by settlers traveling on the Oregon Trail.

With the coming of the railroads, Washington's timber, fishing, farming, and mining industries expanded rapidly. During both world wars, a large airplane industry developed in the state. In the 1940s, Washington became the site of the nation's largest system of hydroelectric power, electricity that is generated by controlling the flow of water through dams.

Today, growing tourism and computer industries are signs of Washington's success in building new economic foundations. While traditional industries remain important, Washingtonians are increasingly aware that their abundant natural resources will not last forever. In the new century, their greatest challenge will be to find new ways to conserve their priceless heritage for future generations.

PART ONE

RICHES OF THE NORTHWEST

This view of Esquimault Harbor, painted in 1857, shows the heavily forested Washington coast, looking very much as it did when the first European visitors saw it in the 1600s.

When the first Europeans gazed upon the coast of Washington in the late 17th century, they saw a land largely unchanged from prehistoric times. Many Indian groups, each with its own complex culture, had inhabited the region for centuries. Soon adventurers from Spain, England, and the newly formed United States began mapping the coast. Word of the region's natural riches filtered back to the East, and missionaries and pioneers traveled to establish settlements in the new land. As more and more people moved in, clashes between these new immigrants, the British, and Native Americans increased.

The First Americans

The first inhabitants of Washington were descended from tribes that migrated from Asia thousands of years ago. They probably walked through the Bering Strait across a land bridge that once connected Asia with the North American continent. Slowly they traveled down the coast and through valleys, finding ways around the huge ice sheets that covered most of the region at that time. As they began to spread out, these tribes divided into two main groups, the Coastal Indians and the Plateau Indians. The earliest American Indian site in Washington dates back some 12,000 years.

There were several dozen Coastal tribes, such as the Chinooks, Makahs, and Nisquallys. They lived on the Olympic Peninsula and the lowlands and valleys around Puget Sound west of the Cascades. Their main source of food was salmon, but they also ate other types of fish and shellfish. Berries, roots, nuts, and fruit rounded out the diet. Sometimes, on a hunt for elk or deer, Coastal Indians would find a whale washed up onshore. Some tribes like the Makahs, armed with simple harpoons in great seagoing canoes, actually hunted whales.

All of the Coastal Indians used the dugout canoe for transportation. The canoes were "dug out," using stone tools and fire, from the trunks of large trees. Most villages were built along streams or at the mouths of rivers so that the inhabitants could float the giant logs downstream to their villages for carving.

The Coastal Indians' settlements were large and usually permanent—sometimes housing several hundred people. They lived in long lodges made out of red cedar planks, and several families often lived together in one dwelling. The lodges were decorated with elaborate carvings.

Because of the mild climate, abundance of food, and adequate shelter, life for the Coastal Indians was easier than for Native Americans on other parts of the continent. As a result, they developed very complex societies. Possessions and other signs of wealth were important to them; the person with the greatest wealth usually became the tribe's leader.

The Coastal tribes honored wealth with a ceremony called a *potlatch*. Someone who had acquired many belongings would invite other wealthy neighbors to his home. In an elaborate ritual, he would divide up his things and give them away according to his guests' rank in society. In return, the guests were obligated to give back to the host a gift of equal or greater value.

Northwest Coast Indians caught salmon along the rivers where the fish swam upstream each year on their spawning runs. This painting by Paul Kane shows the hunters using traps and spears.

9

By contrast, the Plateau Indians of Eastern Washington, such as the Nez Perces, Cayuses, and Yakimas, led much simpler lives. More than twenty different tribes lived in the region between the Cascades and the foothills of the Rocky Mountains. Because of the harsher living conditions, these groups were constantly moving from place to place in search of food and shelter. In the early 18th century, they acquired the horse from tribes to the southwest, which allowed them to cover greater distances and made them more efficient hunters.

The Plateau Indians lived and traveled in small family groups, camping near streams and rivers, hunting deer, elk, and bison, as well as rabbits and other small game. Salmon was an important part of their diet along with roots, berries, and nuts. Because of the extremes in temperature, they built their dwellings partly underground with a roof of skins or mats. Later, the Plains Indians introduced the tepee, and it was quickly adopted as a seasonal shelter.

Perhaps because the Plateau Indians led a less stable existence, each chief was chosen for leadership abilities rather than for how many possessions he owned. A life spent on the move meant that the tribe could keep few possessions. The only real form of wealth for the Plateau Indians was the horse; some tribes, such as the Nez Perces, had hundreds of horses.

Although they had different ways of life, the Coastal and Plateau Indians were in contact with each other. A substantial system of trade, which included food, woven baskets, and blankets, grew up between the two groups. The Chinooks, who lived at the mouth of the Columbia River, became especially skilled traders—so much so that the Chinook tongue became the language of trade between many different tribes. Eventually, with the coming of European explorers, English and French words were blended into the Chinook language.

The arrival of the Europeans would have a disastrous effect on the Native Americans of Washington. Thousands died because they had no natural defenses against diseases introduced by the newcomers. As more and more Europeans arrived in the region, Native Americans lost their traditional hunting grounds and complex ways of life that had taken thousands of years to develop.

This 1847 painting (opposite) by Paul Kane shows a family inside a longhouse, where one woman is spinning yarn and another is weaving a blanket. The Coastal Indians made rugs using the wooly hair of goats and a now-extinct dog type, bred for the purpose.

The Plateau Indians' lives were dramatically changed after the horse was introduced in the early 1700s. This photograph (below) shows a Nez Perce mother with her child strapped to a cradleboard for safekeeping.

Explorers from the Sea

The first Europeans to explore the coast of the Pacific Northwest were the Spanish. By 1600 they had sailed from their settlements into Mexico as far north as Oregon and the southern part of the Washington coast. They were searching for the Northwest Passage, a body of water connecting the Atlantic and Pacific oceans. The European nations believed such a passage existed and would open up trade routes between Europe and Asia. But the Spanish had little interest in exploring the area further and never landed on the coast.

In fact, for almost 200 years few Europeans were interested in exploring the remote and dangerous waters off the coast of Washington. In the late 1700s, Russia turned its attention to the Pacific Northwest Coast, and Spain quickly sent out expeditions in order to claim the area for itself. The first expedition was commanded by Juan Perez in 1774. Perez sailed as far as present-day British Columbia but was forced to return because of an outbreak among his crew of scurvy—a disease caused mainly by the lack of fresh fruit and vegetables in a sailor's diet while at sea.

The next year, two Spanish explorers, Bruno de Heceta and Juan Francisco de Bodega y Quadra, came

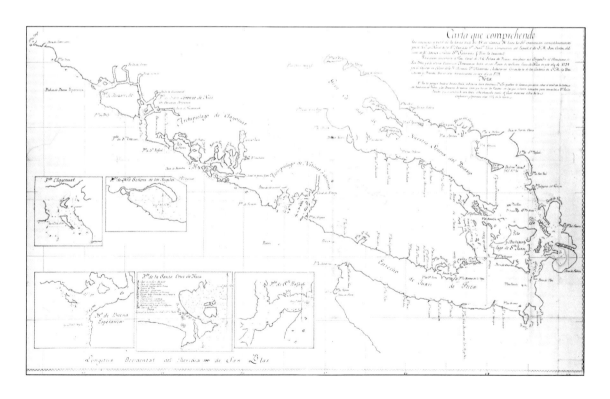

to the coast of Washington. Quadra sent a landing party ashore near Point Grenville. Heceta, meanwhile, spotted the mouth of the Columbia River, but a dangerous sandbar at the entrance kept him from bringing his ship to shore.

In 1776, the British sent the famous explorer Captain James Cook on a voyage to find the Northwest Passage. He sailed along the Oregon and Washington coasts all the way to the Bering Strait before turning back and sailing for the Hawaiian Islands.

Cook's ship returned to the Washington coast the next summer, and, while trading with the Native Americans, his crewmen acquired some sea otter skins. Stopping in China on the return trip to England, the crewmen found that the Chinese were willing to pay large sums for the skins. When British traders heard that sea otter skins could bring huge profits, many came to the Washington coast. The subsequent trade network lasted only thirty years before heavy demand for the skins nearly wiped out the sea otter population.

George Vancouver, who had been an officer on Cook's ship, returned to the Washington coast in 1792. He sailed through the Strait of Juan de Fuca and became the first European to explore and map the great body of water that lay beyond, which he named Puget Sound after his lieutenant, Peter Puget. Vancouver also gave names to other bays and inlets

This Spanish map (opposite) from the 1700s shows the Strait of Juan de Fuca and the southern end of Vancouver Island, with details of five inlets. For more than a hundred years before this map was drawn, the Spanish sailed much of the Pacific Northwest Coast while trading between the Philippines and Mexico.

British captain Sir James Cook (below) explored and charted much of the Washington coast, but bad weather kept him from venturing into the mouth of the Columbia River or the Strait of Juan de Fuca.

that he found. While exploring Puget Sound, Vancouver saw two large mountains off in the distance, which he named Mount Baker and Mount Rainier. The huge island that lies just north of Puget Sound is named Vancouver Island in his honor.

The following year, Vancouver returned to map most of Washington's coastline. Both of his expeditions helped solidify Britain's claim to the Washington area. But an American trader named Robert Gray took an important step in 1792 by being the first explorer to discover the mouth of the Columbia River. Because he sailed his ship several miles upriver, Americans were now able to say that they, too, had a rightful claim to this territory.

George Vancouver (above) first sighted this dormant volcano from afar on an exploring expedition in 1792 and named it Mount Rainier. At 14,408 feet, it is the highest peak in Washington.

Vancouver sent his lieutenant, Peter Puget, to explore the sound that soon bore his name. Puget's party traveled in small, open boats and camped on shore each night. This 19th-century engraving (opposite, top) shows Puget's encampment.

American captain Robert Gray discovered the mouth of the Columbia River in 1792 when one of his crewmen spotted waves crashing over a sandbar. Because of its treacherous currents, rocks, and sandbars, the river was very difficult to navigate, as shown in this illustration (right).

Explorers from the East

As the Northwest Coast became more familiar to the Europeans and Americans, they began to call the area the Oregon Country. This huge region contained most of what is today British Columbia in Canada, as well as all of the present-day states of Washington, Oregon, and Idaho, and parts of Montana and Wyoming. In the 1790s, British and American fur traders began looking for ways to reach this territory by land. Their quest was to find untouched areas where they could trap beaver, whose fur was very valuable in European Markets.

The journey to Washington by land was very difficult. Travelers had to cross tremendous natural obstacles like the Rocky Mountains, as well as dense forests and wide, roaring rivers. The American explorers and traders also had to cross over territory that belonged to Spain—most of the land between the Mississippi River and the Rockies.

The French bought most of this territory from the Spanish in 1800 and, just three years later, sold it to the United States in a transaction known as the Louisiana Purchase. Now President Thomas Jefferson could send an expedition to explore this vast new addition to America.

He chose his private secretary, Meriwether Lewis, to lead the expedi-

Sacajawea, guide and interpreter for the Lewis and Clark expedition, helps communicate the explorers' peaceful intentions to a band of Chinooks in this painting by Charles Russell. The two groups encountered each other on the lower Columbia River in 1805.

tion. Lewis, in turn, chose his friend William Clark to be his co-captain. Jefferson instructed them to search for a passage through the Rocky Mountains and to gather as much scientific information and knowledge of the Native American tribes as they could. The expedition, made up of a handful of young soldiers, set out from St. Louis on May 14, 1804.

Their trip was one of the great overland journeys of all time. The expedition traveled up the Missouri River and then spent the winter of 1804–05 in present-day North Dakota. There they met a Shoshone Indian woman, Sacajawea, who joined the group with her French-Canadian husband. Sacajawea knew many of the languages of the people they would encounter on the way.

In the spring, Lewis and Clark continued onward until they reached the forks of the Missouri River and, in late summer, crossed the Rockies before the winter snows blocked the mountain passes. With the help of some Native Americans that Sacajawea recognized as being from her native tribe, Lewis and Clark were able to cross the Bitterroot Mountains in present-day Idaho. Following this difficult stretch of the journey, the expedition met up with some Nez Perces who gave them food and shelter. The explorers traveled down the Clearwater River in dugout canoes and, from the Clearwater, down the Snake River and into the Columbia.

The expedition reached the Pacific Ocean and the mouth of the Columbia River in November 1805. Enduring miserable weather conditions on the rainy coast, the explorers camped until March, when they headed back home. They finally arrived back in St. Louis in September 1806.

Lewis and Clark's journey was a milestone in the development of the Pacific Northwest. It provided a new route to the West and was proof that Americans had explored the Oregon Country, thus strengthening any future claims in that area. The explorers came back with valuable information about the region's landscape and natural resources—particularly that the lands west of the Mississippi River were rich in beaver and other fur-bearing mammals. When Lewis and Clark's journals were published, many people became interested in the American West and the Oregon Country. As a result, adventurers followed in Lewis and Clark's footsteps, with the fur traders leading the way.

The Lewis and Clark expedition reached the Columbia River in 1805. In this painting (above) by Frederic Remington, the party is shown camped at the mouth of the river.

President Thomas Jefferson directed Lewis and Clark to gather as much scientific data as possible on their expedition. This page (right) from William Clark's journal shows an illustration and a description of a Columbia River trout.

The Fur Trade

The fur traders contributed to the settlement of Washington by providing knowledge of the land, and fur trading became the basis of the region's first economic boom. By the time the Oregon Country opened up following the Lewis and Clark expedition, there were already two large and powerful fur-trading companies in North America. The oldest company was called the Hudson's Bay Company, formed in 1670 in eastern Canada. It eventually controlled the entire fur trade around Hudson Bay.

Over the next century, as the fur traders pushed farther and farther west from Hudson Bay, some of them decided to form their own company. In 1784, a group of independent British and French-Canadian traders met in Montreal and founded the North West Company.

The men who worked for this company became known as Nor'Westers. It was a British-Canadian Nor'Wester, Alexander MacKenzie, who first explored a large part of the Pacific Northwest. He eventually reached the Pacific Ocean near Bella Coola, British Columbia, in 1793. Another Nor'Wester, David Thompson, became the first non-Indian to find the source of the Columbia River in 1811.

In 1810, a wealthy American by the name of John Jacob Astor formed the Pacific Fur Company to compete with the North West Company. Astor decided that the best way to operate was to build a fort at the mouth of the Columbia River. He then planned a string of trading posts along the river so that he could send the beaver pelts, or skins, downstream to the sea.

Astor immediately sent out two expeditions—one by sea and the other by land—to build these posts. The main settlement, Fort Astoria, was

Great demand in Europe and America made the extraordinarily soft and rich fur of the beaver a valuable trade item for the Hudson's Bay Company. The beaver was the main source of income for the huge fur-trading organization, which displayed four small beavers along with two deer and a fox on its coat of arms.

Two trappers remove a beaver from a steel trap in this illustration by Currier & Ives. The trappers would then skin the beaver and cook the tail, which was considered a delicacy in the wilderness.

finished in 1811. From there, the Astorians, as the traders called themselves, branched out into the Oregon Country. They built Fort Okanogan, the first American settlement in what was to become Washington. Fort Spokane was built near the rival North West Company's Spokane House.

The War of 1812, fought between Britain and America, put a halt to Astor's plans. During the war, he was forced to sell all of his trading posts, including Fort Astoria, to the North West Company. Later in the war, the British seized Astoria and renamed it Fort George.

At the war's end, the British and Americans signed the Treaty of Ghent (1814), which returned all captured territory to the previous owners. Although Astor got all of his trading posts back, he decided to withdraw from the fur trade in the Northwest. The Pacific Fur Company had spent only a few years in the area, but it had a lasting impact on the history of Washington. The permanent presence of American fur traders further consolidated America's claim to parts of the Oregon Country.

With Astor's departure, the North West Company was now in control of the fur trade in the Pacific Northwest. This would last only until 1821, when the company was absorbed into the larger and more powerful Hudson's

Bay Company, which decided to move its main base away from Fort George to a spot nearly 100 miles up the Columbia River. Renamed Fort Vancouver, it later became the city of Vancouver, Washington.

In 1824, John McLoughlin was put in charge of the Hudson's Bay Company operations in the Oregon Country. Under his leadership, Fort Vancouver expanded steadily, and as the town grew, company employees

This painting shows a view of Fort Vancouver, the Hudson's Bay Company headquarters in the Pacific Northwest, as it appeared in the 1840s. Located on the Columbia River about 100 miles from the ocean, Fort Vancouver was the center of the Pacific Northwest fur trade as well as an early outpost for settlers coming to the Oregon Territory.

began to grow crops and keep herds of livestock to feed its inhabitants. McLoughlin headed Fort Vancouver for more than twenty years and turned it into an outpost of European civilization, with comfortable residences, fine furniture, and good food.

During the 1820s, Spain and Russia formally withdrew any claims they had on the Oregon Country. This left Britain and America as joint owners of the area, but their governments put off a final decision as to which country should be the sole owner of the region until 1846.

In 1839 the Hudson's Bay Company attempted to strengthen Britain's claim to the Oregon Country by starting a smaller branch named the Puget Sound Agricultural Company. This offshoot, a large commercial farm located near the site of present-day Tacoma, Washington, was intended to take advantage of the increased farming activity undertaken by the Hudson's Bay Company.

By the 1840s, the fur trade began to taper off. Overtrapping diminished the beaver population, while changing fashions reduced demand for the furs. The fur trade, while important to Washington because it initially linked this remote region to the rest of the world, eventually gave way to new enterprises in the region.

John McLoughlin, leader of the Hudson's Bay Company for many years, made Fort Vancouver into a thriving community. Born in Quebec, McLoughlin later became an American citizen and is known today as the "Father of Oregon" for his kindness and hospitality to settlers in the Willamette Valley region.

Settling In: American Missions

As word of the rich lands and unbroken forests of the Northwest reached the east, many people wanted to see the frontier for themselves. Some of the first who came, after the fur traders, were Protestant and Catholic missionaries. Their main purpose in making the journey was to convert the Native Americans to Christianity. They saw this as their religious duty—believing they could improve the Indians' lives through education and by teaching them how to raise crops and livestock.

The first Catholic priests to travel to the Oregon Country arrived in 1838. One, Father Pierre Jean De Smet, set up many missions in Montana, Idaho, and Washington. He became a tireless worker among the Native Americans and was respected by them for his courage and his devotion to their welfare. In the course of his travels, he explored much of the interior of the Oregon Country.

Many Native Americans were curious about the newcomers' religion, believing it was a source of special power for the explorers and fur traders. One group of Nez Perces and Flatheads wanted a mission for their people. In 1831 they traveled to St. Louis and asked William Clark, co-leader of the Lewis and Clark expedition, if he could help them.

When word of this request got out, many Protestants rushed to send out missionaries. The Methodists were the first, sending Jason Lee and his nephew Daniel to the Oregon Country in 1834. Lee established the first mission west of the Cascade Mountains in the Willamette Valley of northwestern Oregon.

A year later, the American Board of Commissioners for Foreign Missions representing the Presbyterian, Congregational, and Dutch Reformed churches, recruited a young doctor named Marcus Whitman to serve as a medical missionary in the Oregon Country. Following his marriage to Narcissa Prentiss, a woman of great intelligence and determination, Whitman prepared to move west.

The Whitmans were joined by another missionary couple, Henry and Eliza Spalding and, after a long and difficult journey, they reached Fort Vancouver in 1836. From there, the men set out to find a suitable place for their mission. Marcus Whitman chose a site on the banks of the Walla Walla River, about twenty-five miles from the Columbia River, known as Waiilatpu, or "Place of the Rye Grass," by the Cayuses. Waiilatpu is near present-day Walla Walla in the southeastern part of Washington.

Spalding, however, decided to set up a mission among the Nez Perce tribe about 100 miles away. The Nez Perces were concerned that the Whitman's mission was so close to the

Cayuse Indians. They believed that the Cayuses were not to be trusted because they were unaccustomed to living with non-Indians.

Whitman sent for Narcissa at Fort Vancouver and the two settled in. They taught the Cayuses, a hunting people, how to farm. Narcissa taught some how to read and write, and Marcus treated their illnesses. The Whitmans had a daughter, Alice, the first child born to American citizens in the Pacific Northwest. However, the Cayuses had difficulty accepting the changes the Whitmans brought into their lives. The differences between their cultures were too great.

Another problem was that Waiilatpu was located on the main route from the East, which would become known as the Oregon Trail. Thousands of settlers eventually used the route to come into the Oregon Country. Whitman himself made a trip east in 1842 and returned to

As part of his work as a Catholic missionary, Father Pierre Jean De Smet (top) traveled widely in the interior of the Oregon Country. Since he was respected by Native Americans, De Smet often served as a peacemaker during their disputes with settlers.

The Flatheads as well as the Nez Perces welcomed missionaries to settle among them. As this illustration of a Flathead boy (right) shows, the tribe did not practice "head flattening"—a custom popular among the Coast Salish Indians.

Waiilatpu with more than 900 settlers. These were some of the first pioneers to arrive via the Oregon Trail. Over the next four years, Waiilatpu became a major stopping point for weary travelers bound for the Willamette Valley.

The Cayuses worried that Whitman was bringing in too many people and that these newcomers would take their lands. In addition, like other Native Americans who lacked natural defenses to the pioneer's diseases, many Cayuses died from sicknesses brought by the new settlers. On November 19, 1847, the tribe rose up and killed Marcus and Narcissa Whitman along with twelve other settlers at Waiilatpu. The Whitman Massacre, as it became known, led to the Cayuse War of 1848–50. Five Cayuses eventually came forward as the murderers and were brought to trial, found guilty, and hanged. Although other missionaries continued their work among the Indians, this tragic incident and the resulting violence brought the main part of the missionary period to an end.

In that short period, people like the Whitmans and Spaldings had done their best to prepare the Native Americans for the rapid changes in their traditional way of life. Yet, for the most part, the missionaries were unsuccessful. Tensions between Indians and non-Indians grew even worse as more settlers came into the region.

William Henry Jackson painted this view of the Whitman Mission (left) in 1845, by which time the mission had become a major stopping place on the Oregon Trail.

Tomahas, a Cayuse warrior (above), was one of the Native Americans charged with murder in the Whitman Massacre. The five accused stood trial and were hanged in 1850.

San Juan Island and the "Pig War"

Tensions were also building between the Americans and the British in the Oregon Country. "Oregon fever" gripped America in the 1840s, and thousands of settlers packed their belongings and headed west for a new life. The Oregon Trail was by now a well-worn route that began in Independence, Missouri, and ended in the Willamette Valley.

The British saw this increased flow of people as a threat to their claims in the area made fifty years earlier by the explorers Cook and Vancouver. They had lived peacefully with the Americans in the Oregon Country for nearly thirty years, but they did not want to lose their foothold in North America. The Hudson's Bay Company still remained a powerful presence north of the Columbia River, while American citizens settled mostly in the Willamette Valley south of the Columbia River.

In 1844, James K. Polk was elected president of the United States. The question of whether American citizens should be in the Oregon Country had been a big issue in the election. Some people wanted to fight the British to make the boundary of the United States farther north, in what is now Canada.

When the Americans and British sat down to talk in 1846, they agreed to a compromise—the Oregon Treaty. It set the international boundary at the 49th parallel of latitude, where it remains to this day. The treaty divided the Oregon Country from the crest of the Rocky Mountains to the Strait of Juan de Fuca on the Pacific Ocean. America's most important gain in the Oregon Treaty was total control of Puget Sound.

Two years later the United States Congress created the Oregon Territory. It was an area much larger than the present state of Oregon, including all of Oregon, Washington, Idaho, and parts of Wyoming and Montana. Oregon City was named the territorial capital.

Settlers north of the Columbia River complained that the capital was too far away and asked Congress to create a separate territory in 1851 and, again, in 1852. Finally, Congress created the Washington Territory on March 2, 1853. It, too, was much larger than today's state. The final boundaries were set in 1863. The territory's first governor, Isaac Stevens, served until 1857.

The United States and British Canada agreed on most of the border between the two countries, however there was a question about the exact border around San Juan Island in the middle of the Strait of Juan de Fuca. Both countries claimed the island lay in their territory. The Americans had a small settlement on the southern tip of the island, and the Hudson's Bay

Company had set up a sheep-raising station in the north. They lived in peace until 1859, when an American settler shot a pig owned by a Hudson's Bay Company employee. Suddenly tempers flared, and both sides called on their governments to settle the dispute.

Fort Bellingham sent soldiers to San Juan Island to protect the American settlers. Their leader was Captain George E. Pickett, who would later become famous in the American Civil War. The British moved their forces into position, and soon more than 1,000 troops were facing each other. However, reasonable officials on both sides prevented any bloodshed. The Americans sent General Winfield Scott to talk to the British and the two sides reached a compromise. The island remained under military occupation, but citizens of both countries were allowed to live there with equal rights. It was not until 1872 that the island was finally declared to be in United States territory.

In 1853, Isaac Ingalls Stevens (top) became the first governor of the Washington Territory. He went on to serve for the Union in the Civil War and was killed at the Battle of Chantilly in 1862.

George Edward Pickett (right) fought in the Mexican War before he was promoted to captain and sent to the Northwest Territories. He was stationed on San Juan Island during the Pig War and commanded the U.S. forces there until 1861.

PART TWO

THE EVERGREEN STATE

This 1891 bird's-eye view shows a rebuilt
Seattle: Two years earlier a fire had destroyed
most of its downtown district. The new buildings
were made of brick and stone.

Washington grew quickly during the California Gold Rush. The gold
mines needed lumber and food, and Washington's forests and agricultural land could provide both. In the late 1800s, the railroad opened
Washington up to a nation eager to tap its natural resources. Rapid
growth followed in the next century: Seattle became a major port.
Huge dams were built on the state's rivers, generating electricity and
jobs. Today, the Puget Sound area enjoys prosperity, but other parts
of the state are suffering. In the 1990s, Washington must find the
right balance between growth and conserving its natural resources.

A Clash of Cultures

After the Whitman Massacre in 1847, relations between the Indians and settlers grew worse. From the Cayuse War in 1848 up to the Nez Perce War in 1877, fighting broke out frequently between the two groups. The issue was usually over land: Settlers began claiming and farming land that the Native Americans had used for hunting and fishing for centuries. By the 1880s, the Indian tribes of Washington had lost almost all of their land and were increasingly forced to live on reservations.

When Isaac Stevens became Washington's territorial governor in 1853, his first goal was to sign a series of treaties with the Indians. For the most part, he had little difficulty reaching agreements with the tribes of western Washington. They were accustomed to living in one place and did not have as much land to give up.

The tribes in eastern Washington had more to lose. Since they lived mainly by hunting and gathering food, they needed large areas of land to survive. Stevens called for a conference at Walla Walla, and signed a treaty with the Yakimas, Walla Wallas, Cayuses, Nez Perces, and other Plateau Indians in 1856. These tribes signed with great reluctance and only after pressure from Stevens. Both the Nez Perces and the Yakimas were given large reservations.

The Plateau Indian tribes of Eastern Washington were forced from ancestral lands and moved on to reservations during the United States settlement of the west. A Klickitat warrior is shown below in traditional dress.

This rough sketch shows the Walla Walla Council in 1855, in which several Plateau tribes signed away nearly 60,000 square miles of land.

Treaties between Indians and non-Indians were often broken, usually because of misunderstandings and cultural differences. Indian tribes did not have the same concept of owning land as the settlers, who came to Washington in order to have their own property. The U.S. government encouraged the settlement of the region by organizing the Oregon Land Donation Act, a program that gave land to settlers who were willing to live and work there for at least four years. Many of these newcomers settled on reservation land, and soon their numbers grew so large the government could not ask them to leave. Tensions often resulted in bloodshed.

Gold was another powerful draw that led pioneers to invade lands set aside for Native Americans. In 1855, the discovery of gold near Colville on the upper Columbia River led to the Yakima War. The treaty that the Yakimas had signed with the United States guaranteed that no settlers would come into their reservation. So, when hundreds of gold prospectors poured into Yakima land, their leader, Kamiakin, vowed to fight. The Yakimas fought against American settlers and troops until 1859, when they finally surrendered to life on the reservation.

The Nez Perces, who lived in northern Idaho and parts of Oregon as well as eastern Washington, also struggled against the tide of white settlement. They had signed a treaty with U.S. officials in 1863, but many bands did not want to leave their ancestral lands. Yet more and more settlers arrived, and, in 1877, the government gave the Nez Perces less than a month to move to a reservation in Idaho. The tribe decided to go, but due to tension brought on by the extremely short deadline, fighting broke out between Indians and non-Indians, and the Nez Perce War was underway. Led by Chief Joseph, the Nez Perces evaded the U.S. Army and headed into the wilderness, aiming for Canada. They traveled more than 1,700 miles through mountains and across barren plains before Chief Joseph made the decision to surrender. "Hear me my chiefs. I am tired; my heart is sick and sad," he said. "From where the sun now stands, I will fight no more forever." They were sent to Oklahoma, and after eight years, the Nez Perces were allowed to resettle in the Lapwai Reservation in Idaho and also in the Colville Reservation in Washington.

Hin-mah-too-yah-lat-kekht (Thunder Traveling to Loftier Mountain Heights), otherwise known as Chief Joseph of the Nez Perces, strikes a formal pose in this portrait. His heroism during the Nez Perce War of 1877, when he led his people on a 1,700-mile journey to avoid capture, made him one of history's great leaders.

Railroads and Statehood

The American Civil War, fought from 1860 to 1865, seemed very far away to the settlers in Washington. Most Washingtonians favored the North, although there were some who sympathized with the South.

Washington underwent dramatic change in the 1860s and 1870s. Improvements in transportation made the overland journey faster and easier. By 1860, there were 11,594 residents in the Washington territory. This number increased rapidly as people came west to escape the Civil War or to take advantage of cheap land. The 624-mile long Mullan Road was finished in 1862. It helped open up eastern Washington and made the town of Walla Walla an important stop as a supply center.

A growing network of steamboat and stagecoach lines meant that Washington's products could be carried cheaply and easily. These new advances in transportation helped Washington's industries, such as salmon canning, agriculture, timber, and mining, grow. The fish-canning industry was located along the mouth of the Columbia River, and, later, around Puget Sound. Farming began in the lowlands around Puget Sound with the founding of the Puget Sound Agricultural Company in 1839. By the 1870s, agriculture expanded east of the Cascades to the Palouse Hills, where wheat and beef became the most important food items.

The first sawmills in Washington were built around Puget Sound because the large forests came down to the water, making transport of the logs easier. Several gold strikes in the territory, starting with the Colville rush in the 1850s, set off big mining rushes. These helped create markets for farmers and loggers in Washington. Towns such as Spokane grew as supply centers.

The most important factor for Washington's growth, however, was the railroad. The railroad companies owned millions of acres of land along their routes. The decision of where to route train tracks could mean prosperity or decline for many towns.

In the 1870s the towns of Tacoma and Seattle competed fiercely for the

East of the Cascade Mountains, agriculture was Washington's primary industry. This photograph (opposite) shows horse-drawn plows on a wheat farm in Walla Walla county.

This picture (above), taken around 1885, shows a Northern Pacific Railroad crew at rest. Many of the workers who built the railroads were Chinese.

prize of being chosen as the terminus (endpoint) of the Northern Pacific Railroad. The Northern Pacific was the first railroad to link Washington with the Midwest and the East. The Northern Pacific chose Tacoma over Seattle, and as a result the town grew rapidly after the railroad's completion in 1887. Then the Northern Pacific's main rival, the Great Northern Railroad, chose Seattle as the terminus for

its line, completed in 1893. The arrival of the railroads meant that the Washington area could now be reached in a matter of days rather than months. For the first time, Washington's raw materials could be moved easily to markets in the East and around the world.

Unlike Oregon, which became a state in 1859 after ten years as a territory, Washington remained a territory for more than thirty-five years. Washington's growth had been slower than Oregon's, but the railroads brought rapid change in their wake. The population of Washington in 1880 was 75,116. By 1890, it had reached 349,390. This was an amazing 365 percent increase in just ten years. Many of the newcomers were immigrants from Scandinavia and Eastern Europe, drawn to Washington by the growing need for unskilled labor. Thousands of Chinese who worked as miners and railroad laborers stayed on after completing their jobs.

Congress finally approved Washington for statehood on November 11, 1889. A few days later, Elisha P. Ferry became the first governor of the 42nd state. Washington was now a part of the United States.

Prosperity on Puget Sound

The same year that Washington became a state, Seattle was almost completely destroyed by fire. A great blaze wiped out much of the downtown business district. The cost of rebuilding was in the millions, but Seattle emerged stronger than before.

Just a few years after the arrival of the Great Northern Railroad in 1893, Seattle had grown from a small frontier outpost to a thriving city. The city's location on Puget Sound made it a natural shipping center for the timber and farm products from Washington's interior. Seattle's shipbuilding industry grew and it began to rival Portland as the most important port in the Pacific Northwest.

This rapid growth was not without problems. Slums developed, and Seattle's waterfront area became notorious for its rough neighborhoods. Tensions arose between different ethnic groups in the city: Unemployed white workers often resented the Chinese, who would agree to work for lower wages. When unemployment was high in the mid-1880s, Seattle

After completing their work on the railroad, thousands of Chinese laborers moved to cities like Seattle, where they lived together in large neighborhoods like the one shown in this drawing. Many started small businesses, such as laundries and food markets, which grew to serve the larger community.

was plagued with extreme anti-Chinese feelings. In 1886, rioting caused the governor to declare emergency military rule, and federal troops were brought in to bring the violent crowds under control.

In 1897, Seattle enjoyed an economic boost when gold was discovered in the Yukon country of Alaska. Almost overnight, Seattle found itself the launching place for miners seeking their fortune. Ships bearing gold from Alaska also returned by way of Seattle. The city's merchants prospered by outfitting the gold seekers with clothing, equipment, and food. Large supply companies sprang up, creating jobs to handle the demand. The C.C. Filson Company, started in 1897, is still in existence today as a manufacturer of outdoor clothing. Even after the gold rush, Seattle held on to its position as the gateway to Alaska.

In 1909, the Alaska-Yukon-Pacific Exposition was held in Seattle to display the city's accomplishments in the first decade of the 20th century. The event drew almost four million people to Seattle. One of the attractions was a new campus for the University of Washington, which had been founded in 1861.

As the new century dawned, Washington's rapid economic gains brought about changes in society and politics. People became concerned about the rights of workers and the conditions they faced in the state's industries. Believing society could be improved by passing new laws, these people and their efforts became part of the larger Progressive Movement in America. Progressive politicians in Washington passed laws to forbid child labor, set an eight-hour work day for women, and gave workers the right of payment for injury on the job. They also introduced new voting procedures, such as the recall, which allowed voters to remove public officials from their posts.

Another innovative law passed by Progressive politicians in Washington gave women the right to vote in local and state elections in 1910. This was called female suffrage, and it was hotly debated among lawmakers and the general public. Washington was ahead of its time: The federal government did not give women voting rights in national elections until 1922.

More and more people in Washington were moving to cities. Many of them were laborers or factory workers looking for manufacturing jobs. Labor unions formed to protect workers from low wages and unsafe conditions. Unions were especially strong in Washington, perhaps because many industries in the state required large groups of people, such as miners, lumbermen, dockyard hands, and cannery workers to work in dangerous conditions.

This photograph (above) shows the Court of Honor at the 1909 Alaska-Yukon-Pacific Exposition in Seattle. The fountain is now part of the campus of the University of Washington.

Women who campaigned for the right to vote were known as suffragettes. The Washington suffragettes in this photograph (right) are posting notices for their cause. Washington gave women the right to vote in 1910, well before the passage of the 19th Amendment in 1920.

Boom, Bust, and War Again

Throughout its history, Washington has been prone to what is known as a "boom-bust" economy. As demand for natural resources like timber or wheat rises and falls, the economy grows or declines very quickly, becoming unstable and causing citizens to worry about losing their jobs. From the beginning of the 20th century on into the 1940s, Washington would experience boom and bust cycles many times.

World War I, fought in Europe from 1914 to 1918, was a boom time for Washington. Seattle's shipbuilding industry did especially well. The war also hastened the building of airplanes, which needed lightweight wood—a boon to the state's timber industry. The Boeing Company, a small airplane producer, was founded in 1916 to help meet the new demand for combat aircraft.

Following the war, there was no longer such a great need for timber. As a result, the lumber industry collapsed and Washington was hit hard by unemployment and other economic problems. The shipbuilding, mining, and agriculture industries also suffered as production levels dropped from wartime highs.

When the Great Depression hit America in 1929, Washington's economy was further devastated. Local unemployment was made worse by the arrival of tens of thousands of farm families fleeing the drought conditions of the Great Plains. Many workers who had steady jobs in the lumber mills, farms, and canneries ended up living in makeshift shacks in slums known as shantytowns. Like many others across the country, a large shantytown outside of Seattle was nicknamed Hooverville, after President Herbert Hoover, who was blamed for the horrible economy.

In 1932, Franklin D. Roosevelt was elected president. He began the New Deal, a massive program to rebuild the country's economy. The New Deal involved large public building projects to provide jobs for the unemployed. New Deal projects in Wash-

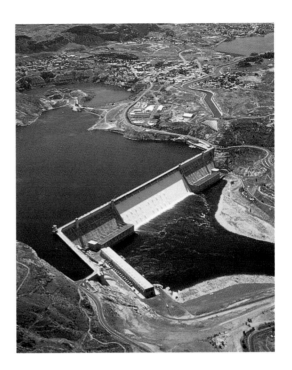

A photograph (opposite) shows women sewing the wings for an early Boeing aircraft, probably during World War I. The wings were made of fabric sewn onto a lightweight wooden frame.

An aerial view of the Grand Coulee Dam (top) shows the massive size of this remarkable engineering feat. The 151-mile-long lake formed by the dam is named for President Franklin D. Roosevelt.

Man-made dams present an obstacle for salmon, who swim upriver each year to return to their spawning grounds. To help the salmon on their journey, dam builders construct "fish ladders," like this one (right) at Rosa Dam on the Yakima River.

ington helped many people through the hard times. They included the Civilian Conservation Corps (CCC) which gave thousands of young men jobs planting trees in the national forests. But the most important New Deal project of all was the Grand Coulee Dam on the Columbia River.

Hydroelectricity is generated by running water through special machinery in a dam. The engineers who designed the Grand Coulee Dam knew that the great flow of water from the Columbia would allow them to build a huge dam. Built between 1933 and 1941, the Grand Coulee is still one of the largest concrete structures in the world and ranks as one of the most ambitious feats of engineering. It is 550 feet high and 4,173 feet long. During its construction, the Grand Coulee Dam provided thousands of people with much-needed jobs. Today, the dam provides electric power, flood control, and irrigation for crops in the Columbia River Basin (the area drained by the Columbia River).

Another New Deal dam project was the Bonneville Dam on the lower Columbia River. Finished in 1937, it provides electricity to southwestern Washington and northern Oregon. One of the special features of this dam was the installation of "fish ladders" for the salmon to use when traveling upriver to spawn or breed. A fish ladder consists of water-covered steps leading up the side of a dam that makes it much easier for the fish to swim upstream.

Today there are a dozen dams on the Columbia and Snake rivers. Together they make up one of the largest and most extensive hydroelectric systems in the world. In fact, hydroelectric power makes up 80 percent of Washington's total energy production.

In 1932, with one third of the nation's workforce—about 13 million people—unemployed, labor unions expanded. Some important labor leaders came out of Washington, particularly Dave Beck, who later served as the national leader of the Teamsters (truck driver's union) from 1952 to 1962. Beck helped settle disputes between the two major unions, the Congress of Industrial Organizations (CIO) and the American Federation of Labor (AFL).

The Great Depression lasted until 1940. When America entered World War II in 1941, the shift to wartime production improved the nation's economy. Because of its location near the military action in the Pacific Ocean, Washington became a strategic center of manufacturing for the war. Washington's traditional industries were boosted and new economic activity developed.

For example, aluminum was in great demand during the war because it was used for the building of airplanes. A huge amount of electricity is required to make aluminum out of

GIVE US **LUMBER** FOR MORE PT's

This World War II poster urges America to step up war production of cut timber for shipbuilding. Washington responded enthusiastically to the call.

bauxite ore. Because of Washington's newfound wealth of hydroelectric power, large aluminum plants were built near Spokane and around Puget Sound. Aircraft companies used the aluminum to build warplanes.

But the most experimental wartime enterprise began near the small desert town of Hanford in the Columbia River Valley, where the federal government set up a top-secret facility to make plutonium. This is a substance used in the atomic bomb and other nuclear arms. The project was so secret that most of the thousands of workers at Hanford had no idea what it was they were producing.

The Rewards of Nature and Trade

When World War II ended in 1945, there were fears in Washington of another postwar slump similar to the one that followed World War I. But as it turned out, the postwar years were good for the state. Washington's industries continued to grow to meet the nation's demands for raw materials and manufactured goods.

The timber industry flourished due to a nationwide housing boom as returning soldiers settled down to build homes and raise families. The wartime aluminum industry remained firmly in place because of cheap and abundant hydroelectric power.

The dam building of the 1930s and 1940s also gave eastern Washington an extensive irrigation system in the Columbia Basin. Water was now carried to this dry region through a network of ditches and canals.

Washington farmers had been irrigating crops since the 1830s, but the new technology allowed more water to go farther, and changed the state's landscape dramatically: What had been semi-desert was now fertile farmland. Today, there are some 1.8 million irrigated acres in eastern, and parts of western, Washington. Eventually the Walla Walla, Yakima, and Wenatchee river valleys became centers of a profitable fruit and vegetable industry. The Wenatchee river valley in the Columbia Basin is the center of

Washington's apple industry, which supplies nearly one third of the nation's apple crop.

All industries enjoyed the post-war boom. The Boeing Company emerged from the war as the nation's leading producer of commercial and military aircraft. Seattle prospered as the airplane industry expanded. New airplane factories were opened in Renton, Tacoma, Everett, Bellingham, Chehalis, and Aberdeen, providing these cities with more jobs. As flying became safer and less expensive in the years following World War II, the airline industry experienced tremendous growth with the development of the modern commercial jet airliner.

Following World War II, the United States and Soviet Union entered into what was called the Cold War. This was a period of tense relations between the two nations and led to a rapid build up of nuclear and conventional arms on both sides. The Cold War also led to the "space race" of the 1960s as the United States and Soviet Union both rushed to be the first superpower into space. Airplane companies supplied rocket parts to the National Aeronautics and Space Administration (NASA).

In 1962, Seattle hosted Century 21, a world's fair that focused on the future. Imaginative exhibits gave visitors a picture of life in the space age while also showing off the best of the Pacific Northwest. The fair drew more than 100 million visitors to the

These giant transmission towers (opposite) in eastern Washington bring electrical power provided by dams to the region's many far-flung homes, farms, and communities.

Advanced irrigation techniques (above), along with the Grand Coulee Dam, helped transform eastern Washington into rich farmlands in the decades following World War II.

Seattle area during its six-month run. The Space Needle and monorail system built for the fair continue to impress visitors to Seattle.

Despite hope that Washington's boom-bust economy could be fixed by high-tech manufacturing jobs, the region suffered occasional setbacks. For example, Puget Sound prospered when Boeing was healthy, but when the aerospace company laid off more than 65,000 workers in 1967 and 1968, the impact was felt throughout the entire state.

As a result of numerous layoffs and a nationwide economic slump, the state's economy was depressed into the 1970s. Washington would have to seek new markets for its goods and attract a variety of industries to its cities.

The futuristic-looking Space Needle, built for the 1962 World's Fair, gives Seattle one of the most recognizable skylines in the country. The fairgrounds are shown in this 1962 photograph.

New Markets, New Challenges

Seattle's trade and shipping industries responded to the challenge of unstable economic times by turning toward new markets in Asia. Natural resource industries like lumbering and fishing looked for ways to increase production. But the limits of Washington's resources were starting to show.

Decades of rapid and unchecked growth resulted in polluted waters, decreased salmon populations, and shrinking forests. People began to realize that increased industrial development was taking its toll on Washington's environment.

Ironically, the increased awareness of environmental problems helped spur a tourist boom in the 1970s. Washington had been a tourist destination since Mount Rainier National Park was established in 1899. But it was not until after World War II and the increased use of automobiles that Americans were able to travel in large numbers. Washington's scenic beauty and seemingly unspoiled landscape made the state a natural choice for vacationers.

While tourism promised to be a source of jobs and income, Washington's traditional industries became increasingly troubled. The commercial salmon fishery, already in decline, was dealt a blow by the 1974 Boldt decision. George Boldt, a federal judge, ruled that Native American fishermen near Puget Sound were entitled to one half of all salmon caught during the annual spawning runs. The Native Americans had claimed all along that treaties signed in the 1850s gave them the right to fish their traditional areas, but the Boldt decision made it legal for the first time.

Since Native Americans were not subject to state commercial fishing laws, non-Indian fishermen called the decision unfair. The Native Americans, on the other hand, saw the decision as long-overdue justice for past wrongs. Tensions remained high between Native Americans and white fishermen, especially after the decision was upheld by the U.S. Supreme Court in 1979.

The timber industry in the Northwest suffered a decline from 1980 to 1989, losing 14,000 jobs due to several factors. Sawmills became more efficient and needed fewer workers, and the Southeast became a new source for timber, taking business away from the Pacific Northwest. To make matters worse, many companies began shipping logs off to Japanese mills, where labor was cheaper. As a result, many Washington sawmills shut down for lack of work.

Loggers also struggled with environmental protection groups. Practices such as clear cutting (the removal of all trees within a certain area) were reexamined in the 1970s and 1980s.

Clearing out vast stretches of forest was a more efficient way to get timber, but it left ugly scars on the landscape and destroyed the natural habitat of thousands of animal species.

By the 1980s, all but 10 percent of Washington's old-growth forests had been cut. (An old-growth forest contains trees that are hundreds of years old.) Many of the remaining old-growth forests were on public land. Environmentalists warned that the complex "ecosystem" that made up the ancient forests would be destroyed forever if they continued to be logged. Timber companies wanted to have continued access to trees on public lands. Many Americans believe national forests should be preserved for future generations and not be sold to private companies.

In 1989, a judge ordered the temporary halt of logging on public land in order to protect the habitat of the spotted owl. This ruling came out of the Endangered Species Act (ESA), which considered the spotted owl close to extinction. The listing was seen as a victory by environmental groups and as a defeat for the timber business.

The issue of protecting Washington's old-growth forests has divided the state like no other issue in recent times. It also points to a growing split between the conservative eastern part of the state and the more liberal west.

In Washington, as in the rest of the country, most of the population is centered in large cities. Most of Washington's population is concentrated in Seattle and the Puget Sound area. Only Spokane in the east has a comparable urban population. As a result, the two halves of the state are frequently divided on certain issues. What is important to a wheat farmer in Walla Walla is not necessarily a concern to a computer programmer in Seattle. The wheat farmer, for example, would be concerned about the price of the water he needs to irrigate his crop. The computer programmer, on the other hand, is more concerned about business competition from California's Silicon Valley.

In the postwar years, Washington voters have tended to elect Republican governors and send Democrats to the U.S. Senate. Senators such as Warren G. Magnuson and Henry M. "Scoop" Jackson served in Congress for more than four decades. Jackson, in particular, was well respected by his Senate colleagues and popular with the people of Washington. Women have also made their mark on Washington politics. In 1976, Dixy Lee Ray became one of the first elected female governors in America. A conservative Democrat, she served for one term but was defeated in a re-election bid.

In Washington, the decade of the 1980s started off with one of the great natural events of this century. On May 18, 1980, Mount St. Helens, one of several volcanoes in the Cas-

The practice of clear-cutting timber to harvest logs has come under increasing criticism because of the drastic effect it has on forest eco-systems, as shown in this photograph (above).

Through no fault of its own, the spotted owl (right) has found itself in the center of a raging controversy over the cutting of old-growth forests. Studies show that the owl may become extinct if too much of its habitat is destroyed.

cades, erupted. The blast blew away most of the mountain's top, leveled 200 square miles of forest, and killed at least sixty people. The Mount St. Helens National Volcanic Monument was established in 1983 so that the public could see firsthand the aftermath of a volcanic eruption.

One of the issues confronting Washingtonians in the 1980s was the changing ethnic mix of the state, particularly the growth of the Asian and Hispanic communites. In figures for Japanese population alone, Washington now ranks third in America.

In one of the most dramatic natural events of our time, the volcanic peak Mount St. Helens erupted on May 18, 1980. The explosion destroyed everything in a wide area around the mountain.

Most Asians live in urban areas like Seattle, as do African Americans. Hispanics were, until recently, mostly migrant farm workers, but more and more Mexican Americans are settling permanently in Washington.

Washington State in the 1990s

As Washington moves into the 1990s, there is a growing sense of limitations, as well as hope for the future. The state's rapid growth since World War II has brought prosperity—and problems. More than ever, Washington is a state of contrasts.

The Seattle and Puget Sound area is fast becoming what is called a "megapolis," a huge, sprawling urban region many times larger than a normal city. From one end of Puget Sound to the other, urban and suburban living space is taking over what was once rural land. By contrast, the eastern half of the state remains primarily a land of farms, ranches, and wide open spaces.

Seattle's prominence has come with growing pains. It is no longer immune to inner-city problems like drug abuse, homelessness, and a rising crime rate—problems that have long plagued cities in the East and Midwest. Traffic congestion, another problem associated with rapid growth, has made the commute to work more difficult.

Today, Seattle has an international feel that reflects its position as the gateway to Asia. And as a regional center for the Pacific Northwest, Seattle has recently seen an influx of young, college-educated, white-collar workers drawn to the booming high-tech industries located there. Many are Californians, fleeing their own increasingly unlivable cities. Access to outdoor areas makes Seattle a popular choice for young, active people.

The break up of the Soviet Union and the end of the Cold War led to a major decline in the defense industry, which touched the whole state. Boeing and other aerospace companies reduced their operations. In 1988, the 560-square-mile Hanford nuclear power plant shut down, throwing thousands out of work and deeply affecting the local economy.

After leaks from hazardous waste were discovered, Hanford became the focus of a multi-billion-dollar environmental cleanup effort. The cleanup sparked a significant economic boom in the area when people were hired to oversee the large operation. The controversy surrounding Hanford grew in the early 1990s, when it was discovered that thousands of people who lived downwind of the site were exposed to harmful doses of radiation in the 1940s and 1950s.

The emergence of Microsoft, a computer software company, as a major employer in the early 1980s laid the foundation for the growth of computer-related businesses in the state. In 1993, Microsoft's sales were more than $2 billion, but while the company has revolutionized the computer software industry, it faces stiff competition from California's Silicon Valley computer companies.

If aerospace and computer industries are Washington's brain, the timber and salmon-fishing industries are its heart and soul. No other businesses capture the romance of Washington's rough and tumble past quite like they do. In April 1993, President Bill Clinton held a "timber summit" in Portland, Oregon, that had important implications for Washington's future. This meeting between timber companies, environmental groups, and government officials was a tentative step toward working out a compromise upon which all could agree.

The current state of the salmon industry, however, has few such bright spots. The fishing industry—in troubled times worldwide—has been hit particularly hard in Washington. One problem is the decline of the salmon population: There are fewer than 2 million fish in the Washington coastal area—down from about 16 million in the 1890s.

The decline is partly natural, but the primary causes are man-made. Dams without fish ladders prevent salmon from reaching their spawning grounds, and the ones that make it are killed as they go over the dam on the way back. Overlogging has caused erosion of silt into the stream. Pollution from farms and too much human activity near their habitat have caused the fish to decline still further. Although the National Marine Fisheries Service unveiled a plan in early 1994 to save the salmon by increasing water flows in the Columbia and

Snake rivers during the spawning season, industry and agricultural groups oppose the plan, and environmental groups view it as not drastic enough. The future of the salmon—a proud and enduring symbol of the Pacific Northwest—is still to be determined.

Most of Washington's development has taken place within the last 100 years. That is a short time span even by the standards of this young nation. The Evergreen State has only recently approached the limits of its vast natural resources. More than ever before, the people of Washington must find a way to preserve a priceless natural heritage while maintaining responsible growth for their future.

Salmon catches as plentiful as this one (opposite) are declining drastically in much of the Pacific Northwest and Washington. Recent reports suggest that nine out of the ten major Northwest salmon species are in danger of extinction.

Washington's scenic vistas attract many tourists who wish to experience the state's great natural beauty. This photograph (above) shows Puget Sound's dramatic rock islands.

Land Area:
68,139 square miles, of which 1,627 are inland water. Ranks 20th in size.

Major rivers:
The Columbia; the Snake; the Pend Oreille; the Spokane; the Okanogan; the Methow; the Wenatchee; the Yakima; the Lewis; the Cowlitz; the Skagit; the Colville; the Chehalis.

Highest Point: Mt. Rainier, 14,410 ft.

Major Bodies of Water:
Puget Sound; Lake Chelan; Lake Roosevelt; Lake Washington; Lake Sammamish; Lake Whatcom; Lake Crescent; Lake Cushman; Lake Quinault; Lake Wenatchee; Ozette Lake; Lake Kachess; Cle Elum Lake; Moses Lake; Lake Ross.

Climate:
Average January temperature: 30°F
Average July temperature: 66°F

Population: 5,135,731 (1992)
Rank: 16th
    1900: 518,103
    1870: 23,955

Population of major cities (1990):

City	Population
Seattle	516,259
Spokane	177,196
Tacoma	176,664
Yakima	54,827
Vancouver	46,380
Olympia	33,840

Ethnic breakdown by percentage (1990):

Ethnicity	Percentage
White	86.7%
Hispanic	4.4%
African American	3.0%
Asian/Pacific Islander	4.2%
Native American	1.6%
Other	1%

Economy:
    Lumbering, agriculture, hydroelectric energy, manufacturing (aerospace systems, wood products, and processed food), fishing, mining, and tourism.

State government:
    Legislature: Made up of the 49-member Senate and the 98-member House. Senators serve 4-year terms and representatives serve 2-year terms.
    Governor: The governor, who is elected for a 4-year term, heads the executive branch.
    Courts: The state supreme court is the highest court in the state, with 9 judges elected on a nonpartisan (no party) basis. They serve 6-year terms. A court of appeals was established in 1969 with 12 judges who also serve 6-year terms.
State capital: Olympia

State Flag

Standing for Washington's forests, the flag is dark green with the state seal in the center. Washington adopted this design for the flag in 1923.

State Seal

The seal for Washington bears a portrait of George Washington. Between the inner and outer circles is printed "The Seal of the State of Washington" and the year of admission into the Union, 1889.

State Motto

"Alki," a word from the Chinook dialect, means "by and by." The motto first appeared on the Territorial Seal designed by Lt. J. K. Duncan.

State Nickname

The "Evergreen State"; sometimes called the "Chinook State."

Places

Birch Bay State Park, Blain

Bloedel Reserve, Bainbridge Island

Camp Six Logging Museum, Tacoma

Cape Disappointment Lighthouse, Ilwaco

Children's Museum Northwest, Bellingham

Children's Museum of Tacoma, Tacoma

Clallam County Historical Museum, Port Angeles

Columbia Gorge Interpretive Center, Stevenson

Dash Point State Park, Tacoma

Fort Canby State Park, Ilwaco

Fort Columbia State Park and Interpretive Center, Chinook

Grand Coulee Dam, Coulee Dam

Hovander Homestead Park, Ferndale

Ilwaco Heritage Museum, Ilwaco

Larrabee State Park, Bellingham

Leadbetter State Park, Surfside

Legislative Building, Olympia

Lewis & Clark Interpretive Center, Ilwaco

Maritime Heritage Center, Bellingham

Mt. Baker Theater, Bellingham

Mt. Rainier National Park, Paradise

Mount St. Helens National Volcanic Monument, Silver Lake

to See

North Cascades National Park, Newhalem

North Head Lighthouse, Ilwaco

Northwest Trek Wildlife Park, Tacoma

Olympic National Park, Port Angeles

Oysterville Church, Oysterville

Pantages Theater, Tacoma

Pioneer Park, Ferndale

Point Defiance Park, Tacoma

Point Defiance Zoo and Aquarium, Tacoma

San Juan Islands National Historic Park, Friday Harbor

Sea Resources Hatchery Complex, Chinook

Seattle Aquarium, Seattle

Seattle Art Museum, Seattle

Seattle Children's Museum, Seattle

Sequim-Dungeness Museum, Sequim

Space Needle, Seattle

State Capitol Museum, Olympia

Tacoma Art Museum, Tacoma

Washington Park Arboretum, Seattle

Whale Museum, Friday Harbor

Whatcom Museum of History and Art, Bellingham

Whitman Mission National Historic Site, Walla Walla

Wolfhaven, Olympia

State Flower

The coast rhododendron, a flowering shrub with pink blooms, was chosen as Washington's state flower in 1892.

State Bird

The willow goldfinch became Washington's official state bird in 1931. A little bird with a yellow body and black wings, it is also known as the wild canary.

State Tree

Chosen in 1947, the western hemlock is a backbone of the state's timber industry.

Washington History

1775 Spanish explorers Bruno Heceta and Juan Francisco de la Bodega y Quadra land near Point Grenville

1778 English captain James Cook sails along Washington coast

1791 Spanish colonists establish first European settlement on Neah Bay

1792 American Robert Gray discovers mouth of the Columbia River
•British captain George Vancouver completes the first mapping of the entire coastline

1805 Lewis and Clark expedition reaches the mouth of the Columbia River at the Pacific Ocean

1811 Americans under John Jacob Astor establish a post at Fort Okanogan

1818 The United States and Great Britain enter into joint occupation of the Oregon region, which included Washington

1825 The Hudson's Bay Company establishes Fort Vancouver

1836 Missionaries Marcus and Narcissa Whitman found a mission at Waiilatpu

1840s First rush of settlers

1846 The Oregon Treaty makes the 49th parallel the border between Washington and Canada
•Founding of Olympia

American

1492 Christopher Columbus reaches the New World

1607 Jamestown (Virginia) founded by English colonists

1620 *Mayflower* arrives at Plymouth (Massachusetts)

1754–63 French and Indian War

1765 Parliament passes Stamp Act

1775–83 Revolutionary War

1776 Signing of the Declaration of Independence

1788–90 First congressional elections

1791 Bill of Rights added to U.S. Constitution

1803 Louisiana Purchase

1812–14 War of 1812

1820 Missouri Compromise

1836 Battle of the Alamo, Texas

1846–48 Mexican-American War

1849 California Gold Rush

1860 South Carolina secedes from Union

1861–65 Civil War

1862 Lincoln signs Homestead Act

1863 Emancipation Proclamation

1865 President Lincoln assassinated (April 14)

1865–77 Reconstruction in the South

1866 Civil Rights bill passed

1881 President James Garfield shot (July 2)

History

1896 First Ford automobile is made

1898–99 Spanish-American War

1901 President William McKinley is shot (Sept. 6)

1917 U.S. enters World War I

1922 Nineteenth Amendment passed, giving women the vote

1929 U.S. stock market crash; Great Depression begins

1933 Franklin D. Roosevelt becomes president; begins New Deal

1941 Japanese attack Pearl Harbor (Dec. 7); U.S. enters World War II

1945 U.S. drops atomic bomb on Hiroshima and Nagasaki; Japan surrenders, ending World War II

1963 President Kennedy assassinated (November 22)

1964 Civil Rights Act passed

1965–73 Vietnam War

1968 Martin Luther King, Jr., shot in Memphis (April 4)

1974 President Richard Nixon resigns because of Watergate scandal

1979–81 Hostage crisis in Iran: 52 Americans held captive for 444 days

1989 End of U.S.-Soviet cold war

1991 Gulf War

1993 U.S. signs North American Free Trade Agreement with Canada and Mexico

Washington History

1848 Oregon Territory is created, including what is now Washington

1851 Founding of Seattle

1853 Congress creates the Washington Territory

1855 Indian warfare breaks out

1885 Anti-Chinese riots result in federal troops being sent to Seattle

1887 The Northern Pacific Railroad's transcontinental line reaches Tacoma

1889 Washington becomes the 42nd state

1909 The Alaska-Yukon-Pacific Exposition held in Seattle

1910 Women receive the right to vote

1928 The capitol building at Olympia is completed

1942 More than 14,000 Japanese Americans are relocated to camps during World War II

1943–45 The secret Hanford Engineering Works produces plutonium for first nuclear weapons

1962 The Century 21 World's Fair is held in Seattle

1979 U.S. Supreme Court upholds the treaty rights of Washington Indians to catch half of all salmon returning to traditional waters

1980 Mount St. Helens erupts

1993 A national timber summit eases tensions between loggers and environmentalists

Seattle (c. 1786–1866) This Indian chief of the Duwamish, Suquamish, and other tribes befriended the white settlers of that region. The city of Seattle is named after him.

Garry Spokane (1811–92) This Indian missionary was a leader among the tribes of the Columbia Basin for almost sixty years.

Arthur Armstrong Denny (1822–89) Denny was a pioneer and author who founded the settlement that was to become Seattle. He wrote *Pioneer Days on Puget Sound.*

Chief Joseph (c. 1840–1904) This Nez Perce chief led a famous retreat through Idaho and Montana in 1877. He eventu-

William Boeing

ally surrendered to the U.S. government and was resettled to the Colville Indian Reservation. A monument marks his grave in Nespelem.

Bertha Knight Landes (1868–1943) Mayor of Seattle from 1926–28, Landes was the first woman to serve as mayor of a major U.S. city.

Vernon Louis Parrington (1871–1929) Author and professor of English at the University of Washington, Parrington won the Pulitzer Prize for history in 1928 for the first of two volumes of his *Main Currents in American Thought.*

Carl Frelinghuysen Gould (1873–1939) One of the leading architects in the Northwest, he founded and headed the department of architecture at the University of Washington.

William Edward Boeing (1881–1956) Boeing was an aircraft manufacturer who founded Boeing Airplane Company. A lumberman and weekend pilot, he predicted the airplane's potential and became a highly successful airplane manufacturer.

Jonathan Mahew Wainwright (1883–1953) Born in Fort Walla Walla, this U.S. Army general was captured by the Japanese in World War II. He was later awarded the Congressional Medal of Honor.

Guthrie McClintic (1893–1961) This Broadway producer and director was born and raised in Seattle. During a forty-year career he directed nearly 100 plays, many of which starred his wife, Katherine Cornell.

Eric A. Johnston (1896–1963) A Spokane businessman, Johnston became president of the United States Chamber of Commerce from 1942–46, and later held government posts under presidents Roosevelt, Truman, and Eisenhower.

William Orville Douglas (1898–1980) Growing up in Yakima, this future associate justice of the Supreme Court was the son of a Presbyterian missionary. Appointed in 1939 by Franklin D. Roosevelt, he was the youngest justice in the country, at age forty-one.

Harry Lillis (Bing) Crosby (1904–77) A native of Tacoma, Crosby briefly studied law in Washington before becoming a singer and an entertainer. He eventually sold more than 300 million records and made fifty movies.

Edward R. Murrow (1908–65) A former student at Washington State College, Murrow became the most influential and respected broadcast journalist of his day, the first pioneer of in-depth television news reporting.

Theodore Roethke (1908–63) A poet, Roethke won the Pulitzer Prize for *The Waking* in 1953. He taught at the University of Washington from 1947 until his death.

Audrey May Wurdemann (1911–60) A Seattle native, Wurdemann was the winner of the 1935 Pulitzer Prize for poetry.

Henry Martin Jackson (1912–83) A native of Everett, this lawyer and politician was chairman of the Democratic National Committee from 1960–61. Jackson also served in both the House of Representatives and the Senate.

Mary McCarthy (1912–89) Born in Seattle, she became a critic and novelist, writing more than twenty books of fiction, essays, and reportage.

Minoru Yamasaki (1912–86) This Seattle-born architect is known for his designs of the Federal Science Pavilion at the Century 21 World's Fair in Seattle in 1962, and the World Trade Center towers in New York City.

Dixy Lee Ray (b. 1914) Born in Tacoma, Ray served as the governor of Washington from 1977–81.

Patrice Munsel (b. 1925) A Spokane native, Munsel is a singer who made her operatic debut at the Metropolitan Opera in New York City in 1943.

Thomas Stephen Foley (b. 1929) Born in Spokane, Foley has been a member of the U.S. House of Representatives since 1964. He was Speaker of the House from 1989 to 1995.

James W. Whitaker (b. 1931) As a youth, Whitaker spent his summers as a guide on the slopes of Mount Rainier. He later became the first American

Bing Crosby

to reach the top of Mount Everest in 1963.

James Marshall (Jimi) Hendrix (1942–70) Born in Seattle, this highly acclaimed guitarist made his U.S. debut at the Monterey Pop Festival in 1967. He was elected to the Rock and Roll Hall of Fame in 1992.

Gary Larson (b. 1950) A former cartoonist for the Seattle *Times*, Larson is best known for his strip "The Far Side." It appears in more than 300 newspapers.

Bill Gates (b. 1956) Gates co-founded Microsoft Corporation, the world's leading software firm, in 1975.

Pictures in this volume:

Amon Carter Museum: 16-17

The Boeing Company Archives: 60

Bonneville Power Administration: 44

Library of Congress: 10, 12, 13, 14, 15 (bottom), 19 (both), 21, 23, 25, 27, 29 (both), 30, 31, 33, 41 (bottom)

Marquette University Archives: 25

Museum of History & Industry: 40, 46

National Agriculture Library: 49 (bottom), 52

National Archives: 7, 34, 43, 49 (top)

National Park Service: 20, 22, 26-27

Olympic National Park: 53

Smithsonian Institution: 32

University of Washington Library, Special Collections: 11, 35, 36, 37, 39 (both), 45

U.S. Bureau of Reclamation/H.S. Holmes: 41 (top)

U.S. Geological Survey: 50

———

About the author:

William Cocke lives in Lexington, Virginia. He is a contributing editor at the alumni magazine at Washington and Lee University, where he also writes for the news office. An avid outdoorsman, Mr. Cocke has contributed articles to local newspapers and magazines, primarily on natural history.

Suggested reading:

Avery, Mary W. Washington: *A History of the Evergreen State, Seattle and Washington*. University of Washington Press, 1965.

Carpenter, Allan. *The New Enchantment of America: Washington*. Chicago: Childrens Press, 1979.

Fradin, Dennis B. *Washington in Words and Pictures*. Chicago: Childrens Press, 1980.

Marsh, Carole. *Washington Timeline: A Chronology of Washington History, Trivia, Legend, Lore, and More*. Decatur, GA: Gallopade Publishing Group, 1992.

Stein, R. Conrad. *America the Beautiful: Washington*. Chicago: Childrens Press, 1991.

Thompson, Kathleen. *Washington*. Milwaukee: Raintree Publishers, 1987.

———

For more information contact:

Washington State Historical Society
315 North Stadium Way
Tacoma, WA 98403
(206) 597-4186

Washington State Tourism
PO Box 42500
Olympia, WA 98504-2500
(800) 544-1800

INDEX

Page numbers in *italics* indicate illustrations